THE VILLAGE SHOP

Lin Bensley

SHIRE PUBLICATIONS

First published in Great Britain in 2008 by Shire
Publications Ltd,
Midland House, West Way, Botley, Oxford OX2 0PH,
United Kingdom.
443 Park Avenue South, New York, NY 10016, USA.

E-mail: shire@shirebooks.co.uk •
www.shirebooks.co.uk

Every attempt has been made by the publisher to secure
the appropriate permissions for materials reproduced in
this book. If there has been any oversight we will be happy
to rectify the situation and a written submission should be
made to the Publishers.

A CIP catalogue record for this book is available from the
British Library.

Shire Library no. 466 • ISBN-13: 978 0 7478 0675 2

Lin Bensley has asserted his right under the Copyright,
Designs and Patents Act, 1988,
to be identified as the author of this book.

Designed by Ken Vail Graphic Design, Cambridge, UK,
and typeset in Perpetua and Gill Sans.
Printed in Malta by Gutenberg Press Ltd.

08 09 10 11 12   10 9 8 7 6 5 4 3 2 1

COVER IMAGE
Now reconstructed at Beamish, The North of England
Open Air Museum, this Co-operative store originated
from the mining village of Annfield Plain, Durham, and
includes a grocery department, a drapery and a hardware
section dating from the early twentieth century.

TITLE PAGE IMAGE
Rationing was introduced in 1940, in response to
shortages brought about by the Second World War. Once
issued with a ration book, each family or individual had to
register with a supplier from whom the ration would
exclusively be bought. The shopkeeper would cut out
coupons for the rations required, the number varying
according to the availability of food.

CONTENTS PAGE IMAGE
Pictured in the early twentieth century, Thomas Page's
shop served the village of Yoxall, Staffordshire, from about
1900 to the 1960s. One side of the shop sold food, while
the other sold domestic hardware.

ACKNOWLEDGEMENTS
Abergavenney museum, p.25; Alamy Limited, p.42 (both),
p.43 (all); Andre Brown, p.44 (bottom); Author, p.6, p.8
(both), p.22 (top), p.26 (top), p.34 (bottom left), p.37
(bottom), p.44 (top), p.45 (bottom), p.47; Beamish – The
North of England Open Air Museum, p.1, p.16 (bottom),
p.18, p.21 (bottom left and bottom right); Bridgman Art
Library, pp.4 and 5; Mark Collins, p.12; Max Fletcher,
p.39 (bottom); Gressenhall Farm and Workhouse –
Museum of Norfolk Life, p.34; John Londei, p.28, p.41
(both); Motco Enterprises Ltd., p.11; Clay Perry, p.40
(both); Plexus Publishing, p.20; The Priest's House
Museum, p.22 and p.24; How We Lived Then – museum
of shops, p.25 (top left); The Robert Opie Collection, p.19
(top), p.25 (right), p.27 (bottom), p.32 (bottom left and
right), p.34 (bottom right), p.35 (bottom right);
Oxfordshire Studies, p.19 (bottom), p.23 (bottom right),
p.30 (bottom right), p.31 (top left and right); Rural
Development Commission, p.21, p.36, p.46; Science and
Society Picture Library, p.14, p.33; Staffordshire Arts and
Museum Service, p.3; Topfoto, p.2, p.31 (bottom), p.32
(top), p.35 (bottom left), p.37 (top), p.38; ViRSA, p.45
(top), p.46 (top); Vale and Downland Museum, p.16 (top),
p.17 (bottom), p.30 (bottom left); Hazel Wheeler / Sutton
Publishing, p.23 (top and bottom left); Weald and
Downland Open Air Museum, p.9 (both) and p.10; Dianne
Young, p.13; Uncredited images, p.26 (bottom), p.27 (top
right and left), p.38 (top), p.39 (top).

Shire Publications is supporting the Woodland Trust, the UK's leading woodland conservation charity, by funding the dedication of trees.

CONTENTS

BEFORE THE
VILLAGE SHOP

Bartholomew Fair by Egbert van Heemskerck (1676–1744). Established at Smithfield, London, in 1133 and originally a cloth-trading fair, by the eighteenth century it had become dominated by sideshows and entertainers. (Bridgeman Art Library)

DURING the sixteenth century the majority of England's population lived a rural existence. Apart from noblemen and churchmen, society consisted almost entirely of the labouring classes. London was the only large city, having a population of about 80,000, while Norwich, Bristol and Exeter were important trading centres but in reality were little more than large country towns.

Almost everyone was self-sufficient. Families of necessity had to grow, rear or catch their own food. Besides being a source of food, animals were also kept for the sake of their wool or leather, from which clothing would be made. Any surplus produce was sold at the local market, where people bought the things they could not make for themselves. The staple commodities for sale or exchange were bread, meat, ale, firewood, candles

and articles made of wood, metal or cloth. It was at the market that the producer and consumer met face to face, an experience that would become rarer as the practice of retailing progressed.

Annual fairs also played their part in furnishing the needs of the nation. Most fairs originated as religious gatherings held at Candlemas, Easter, Whitsuntide, Michaelmas and Christmas, and often bore the names of saints, such as St Giles, St Luke or St Botolph. People journeyed from miles around, often as much to witness the spectacle and partake in the entertainment as to stock up with the supplies they could not obtain at other times. The Crusades aroused interest in foreign goods and so encouraged merchants from the East to attend the annual fairs and to sell their costly fabrics, precious metals, jewellery, Venetian glass, Flemish linen and French wine to those of wealth and status.

Apart from the weekly markets and annual fairs, most villagers relied upon itinerant tradesmen, known variously as hawkers, pedlars, chapmen, packmen or cheapjacks, for their household requirements. These men carried their wares on their backs and roamed the countryside, often covering hundreds of miles in the course of a year. If not always altogether honest, most such traders were hard-working and provided a vital service for those unable to travel to the nearest town. Some became affluent enough to purchase a pony and trap or even to own their own shops. Towards the end of the eighteenth century the increased demand for manufactured goods was better met by the shopkeeper, and so the role of the pedlar diminished. By the end of the nineteenth century most sought to make their living in suburban areas, though many found themselves living in reduced circumstances, forced to peddle baubles and trinkets or even beg for charity.

The Cheapjack by William Henry Fisk (1827–84). Regarded as little better than a vagrant, the cheapjack was a travelling salesman who moved from one fair or market to another. He frequently used a line of comic patter or made exaggerated claims for his wares. (Bridgeman Art Library)

FROM 1500 TO 1860

BECAUSE much buying and selling was done on a seasonal basis, dealers usually preferred to operate from a trading booth, a lightweight structure consisting of a timber frame covered with cloth or canvas, which could be easily dismantled and transported from fair to fair. As the canal system and a decent road network began to develop, so more and more traders abandoned the fair and the market place and took to the idea of fixed-shop retailing.

Possibly the earliest village shops were recorded in the sixteenth century, several of them in East Anglia, most notably at South Creake in Norfolk and Botesdale in Suffolk, along with others in Kent and Gloucestershire. In Lancashire, haberdashers are recorded in Wrightington, Harleton and Burscough, and shoemakers in Eccles, Eskrigg and Ribchester.

There are few surviving shops from this period, though one of the finest is The Butchery at Lavenham, Suffolk, which adjoins the timber-framed guildhall. Dating from around 1520, The Butchery is typical of the open-fronted and stall-like design that most shops followed until glazing became more affordable in the eighteenth century. The wooden shutters are fixed externally and hinged top and bottom. The top shutter could be raised for a canopy, and the bottom shutter lowered and supported on brackets or legs to create a stall-board for the display of goods.

To allow more light into the premises, the arched openings of shops were hardly ever subdivided by mullions, unlike present-day designs. The doorways were often narrow, in order to maximise the frontage available for windows, and often fitted with stable doors to prevent animals entering.

Few, if any, of the early village shops were purpose-built; most would have been converted from ground space in existing domestic dwellings. Fittings would have been minimal – perhaps no more than a chest or coffer in which to store goods and to act as a counter – though some are known to have incorporated shelving, cupboards and tables. It was fortunate if a fireplace was included; otherwise, it is most likely that heating was provided by a brazier, when necessary.

Opposite: Chiddingstone stores and post office, Kent, in 2008. Now owned by the National Trust, the shop was first recorded in a deed of 1453 and was bought as part of the manor in 1517 by Anne Boleyn's father.

These first shops, established in the larger villages, were those of tradesmen such as saddlers, shoemakers, basket makers, furniture makers, butchers, bakers, tallow chandlers, mercers, drapers and haberdashers. Many shops also served as workrooms, where the tradesman made his wares and sold them direct. The inventories of larger country houses and estates show that almost certainly these early shops were patronised to a greater extent by the wealthier members of the community, most frequently those who were profiting from the wool and cloth trade.

In London and other principal cities the simple top and bottom shutter style developed into the 'bulk shop' design, which over time found favour in some rural areas. The bulk shop design allowed enlargement of the window opening with a fixed canopy above – usually of the pent-roof type – with a permanent stall-board beneath, now boxed in on all sides, as opposed to a stall-board that had been suspended on brackets. At a later date, in some instances, this projection was enclosed and glazed to become a bay window for the purpose of displaying goods to their best advantage. Popularised in the reign of Queen Anne, the bow window design evolved from that of the bay window and has come to typify the appearance of the traditional village shop.

By the late seventeenth century England was enjoying a new-found prosperity that encouraged the emergence of a new class of businessman. In the cities and towns there were many men who now sought to develop the retail trade as a more respectable line of work. As middlemen who positioned

Below left:
The Butchery at Lavenham, Suffolk, showing the hinged shutters above and below the window. Fixed-shop retailing began to appeal to villagers, who could now buy in bulk when they could afford it, lessening their dependence on pedlars.

Below right:
View of a house in Water Street, Lavenham, with a stall-board clearly visible beneath one window.

themselves between the craftsman and the customer, they strove for respectability as much as a handsome profit. Contemporary evidence shows that they were regarded with contempt by many, yet there is no doubt they provided a valuable service, and from their fervent endeavours arose the general retailer who began to deal in goods wholesale or gross and so became known as a 'grosser', or grocer.

Many village grocers of the early eighteenth century sold only luxury items, such as spices, anchovies, honey, silk, tea, sugar and coffee, and catered for an exclusive minority. Meat, poultry, fruit and vegetables would still have been bought at the weekly market. However, some shopkeepers attempted to cater for all tastes. Typical of this kind was Thomas Turner, who ran a shop in the Sussex village of East Hoathly,

Above:
A pair of medieval shops with jettied upper chambers from Horsham in Sussex, now re-erected at the Weald and Downland Open Air Museum, Singleton, Sussex. Dating from the fifteenth century, these particular shops remained in use until 1967.

Left:
Interior of one shop in the above building.

9

An open-fronted market hall from Titchfield, Hampshire, re-erected at the Weald and Downland Open Air Museum. Stalls would have been set up here by licensed traders. This type of hall, with a council chamber above, was popular in the sixteenth and seventeenth centuries.

and who endeavoured to supply his customers, no matter how capricious their needs.

Turner, undoubtedly a capable businessman, kept a diary in the form of 111 memorandum books written between February 1754 and June 1765 in which he meticulously records his dealings and the day to day life of a remote village 7 miles north-east of Lewes. From his accounts it is clear that he stocked a diverse range of commodities, including tea, coffee, sugar, chocolate, wine, spirits, Dr Godfrey's cordial (a quack medicine containing sassafras, syrup and opium, and often used to treat colic), bread, cheese, flour, butter, potatoes, salt, fish, bacon, onions, peas, walnuts, cherries, gingerbread, raisins, wheat, oats, malt, wood, faggots, sand, soap, wool, silk, lace, linen, shalloon (a closely woven material used mostly for linings), smocks, wigs, hats, coats, gloves, clogs, rabbit skins, chamois skins, pewter, ironmongery, china, earthenware, brooms, brushes, kettles, beehives, fish-hooks, nails, scythes, needles, quills, pencils, paper, ink powder, tobacco, clay pipes, coffin plates, and shrouds. The majority of items are bought in bulk, even gunpowder, purchased in 50 pound (22.7 kg) barrels – used not just for firearms and cleaning chimneys, but most likely also by mischief makers on Bonfire Night!

At the time the village had an estimated population of only 350, yet was able to support three public houses, a shoemaker, a tailor, a butcher, a chandler and soapmaker, a carpenter and builder, a brickmaker, a carrier, a miller and a blacksmith.

The Old Bulk Shop, Temple Bar, London, dating from the early seventeenth century, was one of the last survivors of the primitive bulk shop design that developed from the medieval shop type; it was demolished in 1846.

Though his business continued to expand, Turner worried about his debtors, though almost all eventually settled their accounts, some by bartering, which was still a common practice at the time. This did not prevent him from occasionally fretting about lack of trade. An entry in 1756 finds him lamenting his reduced income, when he is taking only £5 to £10 per week during a period when he used to take £15 to £20 or even £25 to £30 per week. These worries proved to be unfounded. As a general grocer, Turner certainly prospered better than the other independent tradesmen within the village and was soon able to buy the shop he leased and also the principal public house.

The village shop in Chiddingstone, Kent, photographed in the early twentieth century.

Individual entrepreneurs like Thomas Turner possessed the flair and determination to change the traditional habits of the villager, but some customers were often difficult to please. Writing in the late eighteenth century, Jane Austen found cause to complain about her own village shop in Steventon near Basingstoke, Hampshire. 'I went to Mrs Ryder's and bought what I intended to buy, but not too much perfection. There were no narrow braces for children and scarcely any netting silk; but Miss Wood, as usual, is

The Parris family bakery at East Hoathly, Sussex, in 1905. The former home and shop of Thomas Turner, it appears to have changed little since his day.

going to town very soon, and will lay in fresh stock. I gave 2/3 a yd. [2 shillings and threepence per yard] for my Flannel, and I fancy it is not very good, but it is so disgraceful and contemptible an article in itself that its being comparatively good or bad is of little importance. I bought some Japan Ink likewise, and next week shall begin operations on my hat, on which you know my principal hopes of happiness depend.'

Writing in a similar vein in the 1820s, Mary Russell Mitford describes her village shop at Three Mile Cross near Reading: 'like other village shops, multi-farious as a bazaar; a repository for bread, shoes, tea, cheese, tape, ribands, and bacon; for everything in short, except the one particular thing which you happen to want at the moment and will be sure not to find'.

As these extracts demonstrate, it was frequently difficult to keep the customer satisfied despite the shopkeeper's best efforts, yet shopkeepers were mindful enough to attempt to cater for all tastes.

But, individual gripes notwithstanding, it was the Industrial Revolution, along with the continued enclosure of common land and the removal of common rights, that radically changed the nature of village life forever.

A lesser proportion of the new peasant class were wholly or even partially self-sufficient. Most were now wage earners, employed full or part time by the farmers and landowners who had instigated enclosure to take advantage of rising corn prices. Far fewer were now able to feed and clothe themselves through their own endeavours – a profound departure from the accepted way of life. This shift in village life from self-reliance to a degree of dependency upon others to service their needs marked a significant cultural change.

Traders described solely as mercers, drapers and tallow chandlers were noticeably diminishing. On occasion, farmers, market gardeners, carriers, publicans and brewers, among others, kept a shop as a part-time occupation, though these rarely competed with the grocery store on a serious footing.

Now the ordinary man had to look elsewhere for his essentials and it was the universal grocer who emerged as provider. From the 1820s onwards, village shops began a period of appreciable expansion – a visible manifestation that even John Bull and his wife were now willing to embrace a market economy. Though England was still primarily an agrarian society, the Industrial Revolution had begun to transform the habits of a nation. While prior to 1850 shopkeeping was still modelled upon the needs of a pre-industrial nation, retailing in general was forced to react to the demands of an increasingly affluent society during the second half of the nineteenth century.

FROM 1860 TO 1914

B Y the 1860s at least one general store could be found in almost every sizable village across the land. In remoter regions it was more likely for a woman to act as proprietor. This was a role frequently taken on by a spinster or widow, to help eke out her living, or by a wife, perhaps supplementing her husband's income. Where a man took on the running of the shop, he would sometimes augment his duties with another line of business, as a baker, shoemaker, hairdresser or coal merchant.

In more heavily populated villages the pace of change was quicker. While many early practices were simply houses with added shop fronts, more discerning businessmen now saw the need for purpose-built premises, and so the traditional shop we recognise today began to emerge. Those with entrepreneurial skills turned the village shop into what has been described as 'a department store in miniature' and saw the potential in stocking a vast array of goods – grocery, drapery, haberdashery, hosiery, stationery, toys, hardware and medicines.

Personal service was sought by the customer, who expected the shopkeeper to be knowledgeable on all aspects of his stock. He was expected to have served an apprenticeship – usually seven years – to learn the art and mystery of the grocery trade. The family business was prevalent, with son succeeding father, though relatives were often taken on as apprentices, usually 'living in' at a time when regular and long opening hours were the norm.

Most shopkeepers and their staff worked six days a week and some even opened for half a day on Sundays. The Shop Hours Act of 1886 was the first step in attempting to ensure that those under eighteen years of age worked no longer than seventy-four hours per week, but it was to be many years before the Act had any real effect on young assistants in rural retail, and in particular on those who were living in.

The practice of living in frequently applied to other staff besides apprentices. Often, living in was a condition of employment, and unscrupulous employers sought to exploit their workers without remorse to such an extent that more vulnerable employees became institutionalised.

Opposite:
By the beginning of the twentieth century the age of consumerism had begun in earnest, prompting a desire for luxuries, as evidenced by this photograph of a young girl gazing longingly at the sweets in a shop window.

The shop at East Hanney, Oxfordshire. In the 1901 census George Herman is listed as a grocer/dealer, though the blacksmith's shop next door may have been affiliated to the business. A blacksmith or wheelwright commonly set up an ironmonger's or grocer's shop as an alternative form of income.

Joshua Dawson proclaimed himself to be a grocer, draper, hatter and china dealer, as well as postmaster, in his shop at St John's Chapel, Durham. This photograph is thought to date from the 1890s.

The plight of these individuals led to the formation of Half Holiday Associations and the Early Closing Association, as well as the Shop Hours Labour League (formed 1881), all of which sought to limit the hours of opening. The Early Closing Association was formed from the Metropolitan Drapers Association (1842) and consisted for the most part of shop owners who wished to reduce opening hours, though they knew they were prey to the whims of their customers or to local competitors who refused to fall in line.

These individual organisations met in 1891 to form a National Union of Shop Assistants, Warehousemen and Clerks. The new union repeatedly lobbied Parliament on behalf of its members to improve working conditions

The general store of James Eeles at Bampton, Oxfordshire, in the early 1900s. Besides general groceries, Mr Eeles also sold calf meal and iron goods.

by enforcement. These actions finally resulted in the Shop Act of 1912, which also instigated half-day closing on Wednesdays – a major step forward in terms of recognising the rights of the shopworker. It was also due to the efforts of the union that the living-in system died out in the 1930s.

A considerable part of the shopkeeper's expertise lay in his ability to procure goods in large quantities from manufacturers, producers and wholesalers at a reasonable price and quality. After buying in bulk such items as sacks of flour, barrels of dried fruit and chests of tea, he was required to process the goods before resale to the customer. Herbs and spices had to be mixed proportionately,

The village shop in Uffington, Oxfordshire, in 1910. It was conveniently sited, as many village shops were, next to the public house.

The premises of M. Buglass on the corner of Peggy's Wicket in Beamish, Durham. He was a general dealer who, among other things, sold organs, pianos, phonographs and wallpapers.

fruit cleaned and washed, bacon cured and sliced, sugar cut and crushed, and coffee roasted and ground. The blending of tea called for some element of diligence, ensuring the best possible taste when brewed with the local water.

At this juncture, when goods were weighed and bagged, it was not difficult for the unscrupulous trader to adulterate his stock. Chalk could be added to flour, brick dust to chocolate, sand or chicory to coffee, pea and bean husks or sheep dung to tea. The first Food and Drug Act, passed in 1860 to prevent adulteration, proved to be ineffective. In 1875 further legislation saw the appointment of officials to enforce the law and so better protect the consumer's interests. Bakers, brewers, tobacconists and confectioners were also frequently guilty of adulteration – more so than the grocer – and the amended Act sought to curb this practice across the board.

The customer, by and large, still bought in bulk. The stone, half butt, pipe, hogshead, firkin and tod were the favoured measurements for the purchase of goods, as opposed to pounds, gallons or yards.

As well as adulteration, the fraudulent practice of selling by short measure was not uncommon in the retail trade. The Imperial Weights and Measures Act of 1824 sought to redress this problem but did not become standard until much later in the century. In some areas local weights and measures remained in use until the early part of the twentieth century, but gradually more and more manufacturers began to package and label their own wares, thus preventing tampering by either wholesaler or retailer.

Haggling, higgling or chaffering over the price of goods was the conventional way of doing business. Shopkeepers seldom priced goods, and it was up to the prudent customer to make his own judgement before completing a purchase.

Few purchases, however, were ever paid for outright. Though bartering was by no means as widespread as in the eighteenth century – even if employees were on occasion paid in kind – credit was nevertheless expected and extended to all social classes. The gentry continued to support the village shop, partly perhaps for altruistic reasons, but also for convenience and because they knew they could obtain long-term credit. The middling ranks – the parson, the doctor and the headmaster – took similar liberties, as did the farmer, though he was usually liable to settle his arrears only after a good day at the market. The poor, on the other hand, simply had debts. As they were often paid fortnightly or monthly, or at more irregular intervals, it would sometimes take them years to pay off even the smallest sums, but most shopkeepers were remarkably tolerant.

In terms of his own social standing, the shopkeeper was generally a man of modest status. He was friendly with everyone but had few close friends, though this was as much to do with the long hours he worked as anything else. Saturday was usually the most profitable day of the week for the shopkeeper. Receipts from village shops prove takings on a Saturday would frequently exceed those of the previous six days combined. Takings, however, always fluctuated in accordance with the farming cycle and rose dramatically in villages where seasonal work such as hop-picking occurred.

In order to encourage custom through the door it was in the shop owner's best interests to hold a diverse range of stock. By the 1880s this would have been likely to include spices, barley, oatmeal, sago, semolina, tapioca, split peas, mustard, bird seed and sauces, together with a chandlery section containing black lead, starch, soda, lamp oil, brimstone, carriage grease, bath-brick (an abrasive cleaner), fuller's earth, silver sand, sandpaper and Congreve matches. There would also have probably been a hardware section that may

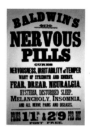

In Victorian times there appeared to be an infinite number of quack patent medicines on the market, with a seemingly inexhaustible number of gullible people willing to believe their outrageous claims.

The premises of S. Warren, a grocer, at Charlbury, Oxfordshire, in the early twentieth century.

19

Ruby Westlake in her shop in Hartland, Devon, in 1976. Her father, a shoemaker, had moved there in 1905 and turned the premises into a general store, also selling electrical goods. He installed two petrol pumps and became an agent for bicycles and motorcycles.

have stocked items such as tinware, cutlery, china, nails, hand and garden tools, adhesive plaster, hair dyes, tooth powders, Seidlitz powders and baldness pomades, as well as phosphorous paste for poisoning rats and bugs. By now branded items had begun to make their appearance on the shelves of the village shop, with some of the most popular examples being Price's Patent Belmont candles, Wright's coal tar soap, Beecham's powders, Lee & Perrins's Worcestershire sauce, Sarson's vinegar, Peek Frean biscuits, Robertson's Golden Shred marmalade, Bird's custard powder and Fry's chocolate cream.

Advances in packaging began to lighten the workload for the grocer. Paper bags, first introduced in the 1850s, soon found widespread use. Some were pre-printed with specific weights, with blue bags for sugar, yellow for dried fruit and white or brown for other items. By the 1880s beer was being sold in hand-blown glass bottles, whilst ceramic pots were used for the likes of hair grease, snuff, mustard, meat paste, ointments and pills. Biscuit tins, as introduced by Huntley & Palmers to aid storage and transport, were gradually adapted to suit other foodstuffs. The tin can, first patented for food preservation in 1810, was also finding extensive commercial use. A steadily increasing number of canned products made their way on to the market, including pears, pineapples, sardines, veal and corned beef, though perhaps the most popular was Nestlé's condensed milk.

Better roads and railways aided the distribution of goods. Local carrier services were quick to make good use of the new macadamised roads, and the village shopkeeper relied upon the carriers to bring supplies from the nearest town or to deliver bulk items to customers on his behalf. Railways were able to deliver perishable foodstuffs, mail and newsprint faster and more regularly than ever before. The development of the steamship brought in cheap imports and opened up new markets. What were once luxury items, such as tea, coffee and sugar, now became affordable necessities.

But the local carrier service could prove to be as much a bane as a boon to the village shopkeeper. Some carriers took villagers into town to do their shopping, or offered to do their shopping for them and deliver it to their doorstep. Soon the more enterprising town stores were also offering a delivery service via the local carrier or their own transport. This was competition the village shopkeeper could ill afford, and those with the means began to offer their own delivery service, either by hand cart, trade bicycle or pony and trap, in an effort to protect their customer base.

A fast-growing population at last possessed the means – albeit in varying degrees – to demand an increasing variety of manufactured goods. The manufacturers themselves soon realised the persuasive power of advertising, and it was not long before walls and hoardings were covered with enamel

Left:
An advertisement dated 1907. The carrier cart service reached its peak between the late nineteenth century and the First World War. Ten or fifteen people could take a cheap, often uncomfortable ride into town – customers the village shopkeeper could ill afford to lose.

Below left:
M. Glister outside his general stores at Dipton, Durham, about to set off on his rounds with pony and trap.

Below right:
R.S. Wilson with his horse and delivery cart outside his general store in Coundon, Durham.

Carrier's Van.

A light-running Van, on springs and patent axles. body 7 ft. by 4 ft., inside measure, to carry 15 to 20 cwt., dripples with hinged seat-boards and portable backs to seats, door at back, boarded top, glass lights in sides and back, portable seat at front with curtains behind same, guard rail round roof, step at back, hay cratch, and American cloth cushions to seats.

£65 0 0.

Extras, if required :—
Pole for two horses, £2 0 0.
Break, £3 0 0.
Lamps, 20/- to 30/-.

Bacton post office and stores, Norfolk. In 1905, its owner, George Webster, who was also a draper and machine vendor, went into partnership to pursue further business ventures, including a boot and shoe warehouse and a fancy repository.

signs and posters announcing the benefits of Bovril, Oxo, Pears soap, Mazawattee tea and Epps's breakfast cocoa.

Improved literacy in the closing decades of the nineteenth century brought a rapid rise in the demand for newspapers, magazines and periodicals. Advances in print technology also helped to reduce production costs, and many popular titles were founded during this period, including the *Boys' Own Paper* (1879), *Tit-bits* (1881), the *Daily Mail* (1896), the *Daily Express* (1900) and the *Daily Mirror* (1903), among many others.

The village shopkeeper soon saw the advantage of acting as a newsagent, a profitable addition to his business that brought in a regular clientele. By the same token, he sought to acquire a Post Office licence to enhance further his worth within the community. From the 1840s onwards post offices became established in rural locations. The invention of the postage stamp and the introduction of pillar boxes helped to promote their popularity. At first the Royal Mail did not necessarily grant contracts to general retailers as a matter of course. Contracts were just as likely to be awarded to the blacksmith, the farmer, the tailor or any other tradesman, or to someone wishing to manage a post office as their sole occupation. However, as the century progressed it became clear that a post office incorporated within a general store was particularly beneficial to both parties.

The post office and stores at Hinton Martell, Dorset, taking delivery of supplies from a wholesale grocer in 1908.

The true entrepreneur in the retail trade now saw the wisdom of fitting out his shop in the proper manner with purpose-made furniture and an attractive frontage to entice the prospective customer. In *Half a Pound of*

Tuppenny Rice, Hazel Wheeler recalls how her grandfather established himself in business around the end of the nineteenth century in a village called Deighton on the outskirts of Huddersfield. Laid off as a grocer's assistant, John Taylor was determined to succeed, and set up business for himself by building his own shop, called Central Stores. He arranged everything in neat rows of tiny drawers, each with its contents displayed on a gilt-edged label: whole nutmegs, Turkey rhubarb, ginger, Gregory powders, sulphur, brimstone, liquorice powder, Beecham's powders, and lots of herbs, including camomile, mint, hyssop and marjoram. Shelves from floor to ceiling housed bottles of Indian brandy, castor oil, jars of Vaseline and tins of Zambuck (foot ointment), as well as washing powders and cleaning materials such as Acdo, Rinso, starch, Brasso, Silvo, Dolly Blue and donkey stones for scouring doorsteps.

The whole family was adept at exploiting their talents for commercial gain. Hazel also recounts how her grandparents converted the scullery into a miniature jam factory and made their own combinations of strawberry and rhubarb, strawberry and gooseberry, blackberry and apple, raspberry and apple, red plum, greengage and Victoria plum, as well as fancy redcurrant and blackcurrant jellies and marmalade, which they bottled and sold in the shop.

In an effort to drum up more trade, they would frequently hold sales to promote interest, and Hazel remembers when 'Grandma displayed some of her drapery wares on the big scrubbed table we ate off, and which displayed the family Bible and picture postcard album on Sundays. What wares there were! Voluminous flannelette night-gowns fashioned to keep out the fiercest winter wind (and Yorkshiremen!); grey fleecy lined bloomers which fastened with a button at each knee and sported a broad band at the waist; heavy and hairy woollen vests with sleeves (one would need to be strong to support the weight to begin with); and pale pink corsets fastened with busks and girded with steel bones to keep the feminine Yorkshire form in trim. They were often as much as 6s 6d a pair. But women, I'm sure, could have

Above:
Hazel Wheeler, author of *Half a Pound of Tuppenny Rice* and *Living on Tick*, two volumes of memoirs that faithfully recall life in her parents' village shop during the first half of the twentieth century.

Below left:
John Taylor, Hazel Wheeler's grandfather, outside his shop in Deighton, near Huddersfield.

Below right:
The village shop in Brailes, Warwickshire.

Strickland's, the local baker and grocer in Three Legged Cross, Dorset, in the 1900s: another example of how a tradesman saw the need to diversify in order to survive.

withstood even the Crusades in those, and returned home without so much as a scratch.'

By the beginning of the twentieth century the general retailer had established himself as an essential element within village life. The village shop had become the focal point of the community, even more than the public house, which relied almost exclusively upon male patronage. Often purposely sited close to the heart of the village, the shop became the place where the locals met to exchange news and gossip and indulge in some measure of social intercourse.

Freda Starr's book *A Village Shop* is one of the few personal accounts of shop life to be published. Describing the early years of the twentieth century, Freda recalls in a matter-of-fact way her life in the north Norfolk village of Cley-next-the-Sea. In 1912, when aged twelve, Freda was allowed to begin serving in the shop, and within two years she was working full time. Even in those days very few items were pre-packed, and most, like tea, sugar, butter, dried fruit and rice, were served loose and had to be weighed and individually packed by the shop assistant. Thick twist tobacco came in hard rope-like coils that had to be cut to length; salt came in bars that had to be sawn to size, and Primrose soap came in half-yard lengths. As many people did their own shoe repairs, leather soles and heels also had to be cut to customers' requirements. Then there was Salazajuice – a strong kind of liquorice used in concoctions for curing colds – which came in rolls about 1 inch (25 mm) in diameter and 8 inches (200 mm) long and had to be cut up with a sharp knife. There were also

A view of the recreated grocer's shop in the How We Lived Then Museum of Shops in Eastbourne, Sussex.

meats to prepare; these included large sides of bacon that had to be cut and boned and made ready in allotted portions of back, streaky, gammon, and so on, and then sliced. These were difficult tasks for a fourteen-year-old girl, most often carried out under the critical eye of the prospective buyer.

All patent medicines were stored in large bottles on a high shelf out of the reach of children and had to be dispensed into smaller bottles supplied by the customer. Castor oil, quinine, sweet spirits of nitre and camphorated oil were all sold by the ounce, though linseed oil was sold by the pound for poultices.

Peek Frean and Co. are now best remembered for their Bourbon and Garibaldi biscuits.

Basil Jones's grocery shop, on display at the Abergavenny Museum, Monmouthshire. Basil took over the shop in Abergavenny in 1906 and the business remained in the family until closure in 1989, after which the stock and movable fittings were acquired by the museum.

The village stores in Sculthorpe, Norfolk, in about 1908, when owned by Lucy Horsley. Like most village shops, Horsley's stores sold drapery and footwear as well as provisions. The village no longer supports a shop.

As most people made their own clothes, a drapery section was essential in most general stores and Freda's shop was no exception. Great rolls of thick shirting, calico, flannelette and all kinds of dress material were heaped upon the counter for close inspection by those drawing out their Christmas club savings. Fine calico for making chemises and drawers was priced at about 1s 3d per yard, and stays, which everyone wore – including children, ranged from 1s 11d upwards. Furs, muffs, feather boas and tippets (a scarf or cape

A view of the interior of Freda Starr's shop at Cley-next-the-Sea, Norfolk, on its last day of trading in 1973.

Two further views of the interior of Freda Starr's shop, including Freda and her life-long assistant Charlie Francis, 1973.

often made from fur) were very popular. Hats were still very fashionable and almost everyone – again including children – wore a hat of some description. Freda's mother had been trained as a milliner and her skill proved to be a useful additional income for the shop. Whereas men preferred the plain style of boaters, bowlers, trilbies or caps, women usually favoured more elaborate headgear, frequently trimmed with feather bands, flowers or ostrich plumes, lined with silk or fur, and held in position with ornate hat pins. Elderly ladies wore bonnets, usually black, but when indoors they normally resorted to a white lace cap.

Invented by Alfred Bird in 1887 for his wife who was allergic to eggs, Bird's custard powder was an instant success!

For everyday wear, most had an apron of one sort or another. In the home women often wore a simple black Dutch apron that cost only a few pence to make. Large cooking aprons cost about 1 shilling to 1s 6d, whilst servants' aprons about 2s 6d. Children regularly wore pinafores, and special occasions usually called for a new 'pinny' that cost much the same as a servant's apron.

Shops hours could be long and tedious: Freda Starr's shop stayed open until 7 p.m. on Mondays, Tuesdays and Wednesdays, 5 p.m. on Thursdays, but 8.30 p.m. on Fridays and 10.30 p.m. on Saturdays. It was a relief to many like Freda when the Shops Early Closing Act was introduced after the First World War and restricted opening hours. Freda's own shop, like others, began to close at 6 p.m., and earlier in the winter months.

FROM 1914 TO THE
PRESENT DAY

A s with most businesses, village shops suffered during the First World War and the years that immediately followed, and, for many, trade either stagnated or declined. Food shortages inflated prices to prohibitive levels. By November 1916 it was estimated that prices had risen by 78 per cent since the beginning of the war, and by November 1918 they had risen by an estimated 133 per cent.

Yet despite the tragedy of the First World War and the adverse effects of the National Strike and the Great Depression, the inter-war years proved to be a period of unprecedented change within the retail trade. During this time village shopkeepers had to face some real challenges to the survival of their businesses, with the continued expansion of the co-operative societies, multiple shops and department stores.

Built upon the work of the Rochdale Pioneers and other co-operative unions, the Co-operative Wholesale Society (CWS), founded in 1872, soon established a nationwide chain whose collective strength lay in bulk purchasing and distribution. Thomas Lipton founded his first multiple shop in 1871 and, like the CWS, he understood the importance of fixed price retailing. His standards of quality and service proved so popular that Home & Colonial Stores Ltd, the Maypole Dairy Company, the International Tea Company (later International Stores) and John Sainsbury soon followed his example. Brightly lit and stylishly decorated department stores such as Clark & Debenham, Peter Robinson and Swan & Edgar also followed suit.

Between the wars these companies further consolidated their success by offering ever more mass-produced items at affordable prices. The country dweller was enticed into the town by these products, which began to raise their aspirations. Perhaps even more significantly, people began to shop for pleasure, and what was once a necessity now became more often a pastime.

By the 1930s the village shopkeeper found it progressively more difficult to deal with competition on such a scale. The department stores and mail-order companies took away much of his drapery and haberdashery trade, while the multiple shops offered a broader choice of stock at bargain prices,

Opposite:
The provision store of Bill Platt in Louth, Lincolnshire, in 1982. Bill's father was sent, aged fourteen, to be apprenticed to the trade in 1894 and was one of the last to sign indentures. Bill took over the shop in 1926 and retired in 1986.

Top left:
The post office and stores in Cocking, West Sussex.

Top right:
The author's family's stores at South Creake, Norfolk, in the late 1920s. The family moved away in about 1930, though the shop continued to trade until about 1960, when it was turned into a private dwelling.

and the co-operatives often swallowed up the independent retailers as they continued to expand nationwide.

Buses also played a considerable part in undermining the security of the shopkeeper. The first service was introduced in 1898, and the first rural service the following year. By 1930 a comprehensive network of bus companies served the entire country, encouraging the villager to seek alternative shopping opportunities.

These challenges notwithstanding, many village shopkeepers continued to survive and thrive, and so adapted to modern retailing practices. Personal service still counted for much, even though more and more produce came pre-packed, reducing the need for the specialised skills of the tradesman. His knowledge of book-keeping and maintaining stock records, however, was more critical than ever before as consumers now bought goods in smaller quantities and more frequently, and demanded greater choice.

A fine example of a village shop, in Longworth, Oxfordshire, in 1930.

The post office and stores in Swerford, Oxfordshire, in about 1930.

If the shopkeeper was ever in doubt, there was always an army of salesmen and company representatives willing to offer advice on stock control and how best to display goods to the advantage of both buyer and seller. It was imperative for the producer and manufacturer to ensure their heavily advertised products were promoted correctly and that the grocer was well briefed. There was now a perceptible shift in the psychology of the consumer to reject local produce in favour of branded goods.

During this period home baking and home cooking declined while the production and processing of foodstuffs accelerated dramatically. A growing number of housewives were willing and able to pay for prepared foods in one form or another; Keillor jam, Anchor butter, Hovis bread, Kellogg's cornflakes, Chivers jellies, Heinz baked beans, Atora beef suet, Brown & Poulson's cornflour and Marmite all made their way into the pantry. Certainly the choice and quality of pre-packaged foods improved during the inter-war years. The growing power of advertising – aided by radio and the

Top left:
Deddington post office and stores, Oxfordshire. The year is 1935, as the posters declare that Italy has invaded Ogaden in Abyssinia. There is a chocolate bar dispensing machine on the wall, and advertisements for Stickphast paste.

Top right:
Kingham post office and stores, Oxfordshire, in the 1930s. This remote village still retains a sizable village shop.

Left:
The village shop that incorporated a post office benefited from additional income and was better able to compete with rivals. A customer who came in to use the post office was likely to make purchases from the range of goods on offer.

31

The salesman was the link between the manufacturer and retailer. While promoting his own products, he could nevertheless advise on selling techniques, window display and interior layout. He would provide promotional material and give guidance on stocking and pricing.

cinema – shaped people's attitudes towards brands that became associated with an improved standard of living.

There was also a developing awareness of healthier eating, with more people eating fresh fruit and vegetables than ever before, though fewer had the means or desire to grow their own. Farm produce shops also began to appear around this time to cater for these needs, and often specifically for the burgeoning tourist trade, which also benefited the general retailer. Hiking, cycling, camping, caravanning and sailing all became appealing leisure activities and it was sound business sense for the shopkeeper to stock a selection of maps, guidebooks, postcards and souvenirs to exploit this market.

It was always necessary for the shopkeeper to search for profitable ways to vary his stock and introduce new lines where feasible. The wireless proved to be a fortunate invention for many rural shopkeepers. Several sold crystal sets and later valve radios, or they supplied a range of spares or offered a service recharging accumulator batteries. Some sold gramophones, or perhaps records or sheet music, or at the very least tins of replacement needles.

Some go-ahead retailers in larger villages also sold sewing machines. The American Singer Sewing Machine Company produced some of the more popular models at their factories in Scotland, although there were British manufacturers such as Vickers Ltd and the Franklin Sewing Machine Company, as well as cheaper imports.

Sales of bicycles increased appreciably during the inter-war years and they became a lucrative sideline for many retailers. Since its invention in the 1880s the safety bicycle had undergone many refinements, achieving mass

An assortment of tins of cocoa, drinking chocolate and custard powder from between the wars. Drinking chocolate contains cocoa butter, whereas cocoa does not and is therefore less fattening. Once, both were as popular as tea and coffee, but their status declined throughout the twentieth century.

Happy campers on holiday. Tourism increased dramatically between the wars and many village shops took advantage of this trade by selling maps, guidebooks, souvenirs and even hiking and camping equipment, or by offering cycle, car or boat hire.

A view of the reconstructed 1930s village shop at the Roots of Norfolk museum in Gressenhall, where a recorded voice informs the visitor: 'Oh yes! I stock everything you're likely to need – all the year round…'

popularity in the 1930s, and for most people it was the first mechanical mode of transport that gave them the means for independent travel. Many shopkeepers who offered bicycles for sale – or also for hire if there was a robust tourist trade – also offered a repair and maintenance service, whilst almost every village store sold a selection of spares or, at least, puncture repair kits.

An expensive item such as a sewing machine, radio or bicycle would probably have been paid for on an instalment plan rather than a hire purchase agreement, although some shopkeepers no doubt preferred the legal security of the latter.

The gentry had for the most part deserted the village shop. In the aftermath of the First World War numerous country estates were dispersed, while many of the families that remained now owned a car and preferred to shop elsewhere, as did a number of the middle class, who had also gained mobility. Car ownership amounted to fewer than three million in 1938, though it is certain the trend had some impact upon the village shop. Some of the better-off shopkeepers now owned a car or van and were keen to offer a delivery service further afield in their efforts to secure new custom.

Following the outbreak of the Second World War in September 1939, the imposition of rationing in January 1940 caused further complications for the village shopkeeper, as it did for other small businessmen. By 1941 the weekly allowance for each adult amounted to 4 ounces (113 grams) of ham or bacon,

Each ration book gave exact details of the food each individual was entitled to weekly. Adults were issued with a buff ration book, while expectant women, nursing mothers and small children got a green one, entitling them to extra rations, and children between five and sixteen had a blue one.

Packaged products available during the Second World War, including dried egg and dried milk powder. The sinking of almost a million tons of food and animal feed in the opening months of the war forced Churchill to implement rationing in 1940.

8 ounces (227 grams) of sugar, 2 ounces (57 grams) of tea, 2 ounces of jam, and 8 ounces of fats, comprising no more than 2 ounces of butter, 1 ounce (28 grams) of cheese and 6 ounces (170 grams) of meat. In December 1941 the Board of Trade introduced a points scheme to control the sale of foods that were not rationed but were nevertheless in short supply. Each person was allowed sixteen points per month and these could be to purchase items such as tinned meat, fish, fruit, condensed milk, rice and breakfast cereal.

The abolition of the basic civilian petrol ration in 1942 curtailed the movement of the majority of people out of the village. Until the end of the war almost everyone became dependent again upon the local shop for their supplies. During this period of shortages there were a number of unscrupulous producers and retailers willing to operate a black market system, selling items such as eggs, butter, cheese or meat 'under the counter' to favoured customers.

Often the influx of servicemen, evacuees and Land Army girls into the village placed demands upon the shopkeeper that he was unable to satisfy, owing to shortages and the need to placate his regulars. The government also strictly controlled prices and profit margins, and discouraged any diversity in trading between wholesalers and retailers.

After the war and the cessation of rationing in the early 1950s, life in England quickly returned to normal. The nation was eager to shake off the drabness of the previous decade and looked to the future with an air of optimism.

An example of self-promotion by the author's father. Calendars were given away at Christmas to regular customers and suppliers. The car-hire service was a surprising sideline but few people then owned a car and it provided additional income.

This village shop, photographed in the early 1950s, acted as a public library for one day each week, a common practice until the introduction of mobile libraries. Some shops also collected and delivered prescriptions for the elderly and infirm.

Lyons tea blends were often named after colours such as White label, Red label, Yellow label and Green label. Once a popular brand, they promoted their products with the slogan 'A packet for every pocket.'

Bank statements from the general store owned by the author's parents indicate how brisk trade was during this post-war period between 1952 and 1955. Located in the remote Norfolk village of Norton Subcourse, the store included a separate bicycle shop and also a petrol pump – one of the very few in the vicinity at the time. The main store, built just before the outbreak of war, was a model of cleanliness and hygiene, fitted out with modern display cases, and with storage racks and a rear storeroom that included refrigeration units for frozen food and ice cream, products that were becoming increasingly popular at the time. Groceries were sourced from a number of wholesalers and provision merchants, while some producers such as Lyons & Company, McVitie & Price, Cerebos, Oxo, Meredith & Drew, Huntley & Palmers and Sarsons still delivered their own. Lever Brothers and Colgate Palmolive appear to have supplied most of the detergents and toiletries, while stationery, hardware, footwear, pet food and similar items were supplied by local businesses in the nearby towns.

Tobacco accounted for a surprisingly large percentage of sales, between £50 and £100 per month. But petrol sales, even more surprisingly, amounted to between £60 and £70 per month. Sales of cycles and spares ranged between £10 and £20 per month and, along with petrol sales, were a sure sign that more and more people were becoming mobile in one way or another. Of course, as was to be expected, this new mobility allowed them to do a proportion of their shopping in the town as opposed to the village shop.

As farming became extensively mechanised and the traditional country trades continued to disappear, so more people sought employment elsewhere. This migrating workforce also had an appreciable effect on the takings of the village shop. So too did the introduction of self-service stores by the Co-operative Wholesale Society in 1942, quickly followed by the other major multiples in the 1940s and 1950s.

A village general store photographed in the 1950s.

The self-service store revolutionised grocery shopping from the 1950s onwards and the village shopkeeper was forced to fall in line. Self-service demanded a predominance of pre-packaged merchandise, individually priced, to allow customers to make their own selection.

Originating in the United States, the self-service store was an innovation that entirely changed the concept of shopping. These supermarkets, as they soon became known, rapidly proliferated in towns up and down the country, providing more shelf space and consequently more choice, yet incurring negligible labour costs. The anonymity of the supermarket appealed to customers, as did the freedom to browse and select products without intervention from the shopkeeper.

Village shops in general followed the lead set by the supermarkets and gradually introduced self-service. The days of entering the village store and

A fine example of a Spar shop in Stradbroke, Suffolk.

The village shop in Clun, Shropshire, in the 1960s. There is little in this photograph to suggest that it does not date from fifty years earlier.

A village shop interior from the 1970s.

A village shop in Essex, 1970.

being offered a seat whilst receiving the individual attention of the shopkeeper were already numbered. Nevertheless, many shop owners were keen to take on the supermarkets and so enlisted the support of voluntary wholesaling groups such as Mace, Spar, VG, Londis, Nisa, Alldays and Circle K.

These groups promoted recognised brands and gave the independent grocer the benefits of better purchasing power as well as allowing him to participate in marketing initiatives. But, as time went on, distribution to the remoter regions proved less cost-effective for some wholesaling groups, who switched to concentrating on larger, suburban developments.

Edith Gibson in 1975, behind the counter of her shop in Hullion on Rousay, Orkney, which she ran with her husband. The shop had been in business for at least 150 years when it closed in 1990.

39

The village shop at Rolvenden, Kent, in the 1980s. The shop is today as much a mainstay of the village as ever, selling a wide variety of local produce from honey to beer to plants.

But no matter how well intentioned all these co-operatives might be, none could halt the decline of the rural shop, and from the 1940s onwards village shops began to close with alarming regularity. By 1979, 44 per cent of villages in Dorset were without a shop and only 10 per cent had more than one shop, while in Nottinghamshire over 40 per cent of villages had no shop at all, and 10 per cent of those villages had lost stores within the previous five years. These statistics were repeated across Britain with monotonous consistency – unequivocal evidence that fewer people were shopping at the village store.

One of the main factors in the decline was the depopulation of villages from the 1880s through to the 1970s, their inhabitants drawn to the surrounding towns and cities by better pay and living conditions. Thereafter, and up to the present, new housing developments have caused many villages to grow in size, but many of the newcomers are commuters, often working

Laxfield, Suffolk, in the late 1980s. This was one of the last shops that traded as a grocer's and draper's. It closed in 1992, when the proprietor retired, aged seventy-six, and it was demolished soon after.

Ray Millianer beside his mobile shop in Tylorstown in south Wales in 1982. Once, Ray did a good trade in fresh fish and fruit, but he later concentrated on sweets, biscuits, pop and crisps. Mobile shops detracted from the profitability of village shops, until rising costs put many out of business in the late twentieth century.

The Post Office Stores, Nant Gwynant, Snowdonia, in 1984. John Dean, a former accountant, took over the shop and, besides selling general groceries, operated an off-licence and sold hiking accessories. Unfortunately, John could not make the venture pay and the shop closed two years later.

41

Low Bradfield, Yorkshire, photographed in the 1990s. Now called the Postcard Cafe and Stores, the shop, besides selling basic groceries, offers organic, vegetarian and fair-trade items and a fine selection of cheeses; it also provides a variety of other services.

husbands and wives, who prefer to do their shopping in town. Some villagers are reluctant to use the local store because they no longer perceive it as fashionable or suitable for their needs. But price is invariably the leading issue. Most refuse to use the shop as almost every purchase is judged upon price instead of quality.

The abandonment of resale price maintenance in 1964 (price maintenance was partially introduced in the 1890s and extended to cover provisions in 1914) meant the small retailer could no longer compete on price with the multiples. Where the average village shop was making 20 per cent net profit per year soon after the Second World War, by the early 1990s it was fortunate if it was making between 5 and 8 per cent.

The multiple stores have continued to expand at an unprecedented rate, with hypermarkets opening in out-of-town retail parks. These stocked almost every conceivable item of merchandise under one roof, have encouraged one-stop shopping. By 2006 Tesco, Asda, Sainsbury's and Morrisons had gained 74.4 per cent of the grocery market, with other multiples and co-operatives taking 22.7 per cent, leaving the independent sector with just 2.9 per cent. The notion of grocery shopping being a social ritual – often conducted on a daily basis – has been supplanted by the proliferation of these

Llangunllo community shop in Powys, Wales, in 2002. After the local shopkeeper died, a community shop was set up in one room of the village pub. When the pub closed in 2007, the shop was resited in the village hall with the aid of the Powys Association of Voluntary Organisations.

The general store, post office and delicatessen in Alfriston, Sussex, a village popular with tourists, in 2005. The store sells home-baked cakes and pies, as well as its own sandwiches and rolls, and local farm-fresh meat.

Lurgashall shop, Sussex, in 2005. This village of over seven hundred inhabitants remains a thriving community with a shop that enjoys strong support from people in the village and the surrounding area.

Sub-postmaster Ron Scott with a customer at the door of his shop in Monkton Farleigh, Wiltshire, in 2006. With the aid of villagers, Ron was twice able to save the shop from closure by the Post Office and it continues to trade.

Above:
Emmett's store in Peasenhall, Suffolk, has been a family business since at least 1840. Once a general village shop, it now concentrates on hams and bacons cured on the premises, and other specialist fare. Some of the enamel signs are original.

megastores, which bear closer resemblance to a factory warehouse than to anything as comforting or inviting as the village shop.

The modern village shopkeeper understands the benefits of stock diversity, and the need to offer other specialised services and produce to

The village shop in Thornton-le-Dale, Yorkshire, has a pharmacy next door.

Winster village shop, Derbyshire. This shop, like many others, was saved from closure with help from ViRSA and continues to serve the community, thanks to a dedicated staff of volunteers.

attract custom, but the struggle for the individual retailer to compete with the chain stores has become an increasingly uneven battle. Independent retailers are shutting up shop at the rate of three hundred a year – a frightening statistic when one considers how adversely this affects the whole community and other traders within the vicinity.

Yet all is not lost. There is help at hand through the Rural Shops Alliance (RSA) and the Village Retail Services Association (ViRSA), two professional organisations dedicated to supporting the independent retailer.

Below:
The post office and general store in the village of Somerleyton, Suffolk, has the added attraction of a pleasant tea garden.

The interior of the village shop in Sulgrave, Northamptonshire, another shop that received essential support from ViRSA. After the previous shop closed, the community purchased a small cottage and, with the aid of sixty volunteers, has turned it into a successful enterprise.

Formed in 2001, the RSA is a countrywide trade association that operates on behalf of the village shopkeeper. It works in collaboration with its commercial sponsors and various associate members such as rural community councils and county councils to offer assistance to the individual shopkeeper on how best to optimise business potential and plan for the future. As a national voice for over 7,200 village shops across England, the RSA is able to lobby government to better protect their interests.

ViRSA – an activity of the Plunkett Foundation – is a national charity founded in 1992. It is dedicated to assisting those who wish to retain or

Promotional material issued by CoSIRA (Council for Small Industries in Rural Areas), which became the Rural Development Commission in the 1990s. The message is the same now as then: the village shop can survive only if villagers support it by shopping there.

The service station with a forecourt shop or minimart often serves several neighbouring villages that can no longer support their own shops. Many such stores sell a wide range of merchandise because they cater for a regular clientele as well as continuous passing trade.

establish a village shop and can offer guidance on how to apply for grants and donations. To date, ViRSA has helped to set up and run 170 community-owned shops, usually operated on a rota with volunteers and perhaps one or two full-time paid staff. Where the community-run shop is the only viable option, ViRSA is always willing to offer practical advice without charge.

The RSA and ViRSA are both organisations that have repeatedly proved to be a lifeline to a village wishing to preserve its community identity. Where once the village shop was the heart of the community, it is now the community that is the heart of the village shop.

INDEX

Page numbers in italic refer to illustrations